LITTLE BOOK OF

Chloé

First published in 2024 by Welbeck
An Imprint of HEADLINE PUBLISHING GROUP

1

Cataloguing in Publication Data is available from the British Library

ISBN 978 1 80279 762 6

Printed and bound in China by Leo Paper

HEADLINE PUBLISHING GROUP
An Hachette UK Company
Carmelite House
50 Victoria Embankment
London EC4Y 0DZ

www.headline.co.uk
www.hachette.co.uk

LITTLE BOOK OF

Chloé

The story of the iconic fashion house

CAROLINE YOUNG

WELBECK

Contents

Introduction

From banana print tops and pineapple swimsuits, to the Paddington bag and the Susanna boots, Chloé's iconic pieces have habitually inspired a cultish devotion. But it's not just the "It" items that people clamour for. Ever since Chloé was first founded in 1952, bohemian femininity has been its signature, giving rise to the concept of the Chloé woman, who is independent and free, possessing an innate sense of style.

The fashion house quickly came to represent the effortless style of the Parisian woman. With early collections held at the Left Bank establishments of Café de Flore, Brasserie Lipp and Closerie des Lilas, it showcased a particular brand of hip elegance – the breezy dresses, the tailored suits with delicate sexy camisoles, the hand-painted silks, the flouncing blouses and shimmering evening gowns.

Chloé's founder, Gaby Aghion, was the original driving force, creating the maison as a response to her belief in freeing women from the confines of couture, which was both physically restrictive and inaccessible to many. She wanted to give women luxury clothing at a more accessible level. It was even said that she invented the term "prêt-à-porter", or "ready-to-wear", at a time

OPPOSITE The breezy, boho feel of this dress by Clare Waight Keller, Autumn/Winter 2016, is the essence of the Chloé girl.

when fashion was ruled by made-to-measure couturiers.

One of the unique features of Chloé is its rotation of burgeoning designers whose talents were able to flourish at the Maison. With Karl Lagerfeld at the helm throughout the 1970s, Chloé built a reputation as the ready-to-wear fashion house for the coolest woman at the party. While there have been other male creative directors, it found its focus from the 2000s as a female-led fashion house. Other designers include Martine Sitbon, Stella McCartney, Phoebe Philo, Hannah MacGibbon, Clare Waight Keller, Natacha Ramsay-Levi, Gabriela Hearst and Chemena Kamali.

Across the decades, Chloé has been a fashion house for It girls for the freedom and the sexiness of its clothing and accessories. In the 1970s, disciples were model Pat Cleveland, actress Stéphane Audran, Caroline of Monaco, Jerry Hall and Paloma Picasso; Kate Moss rocked the maison under Stella McCartney; Phoebe Philo's designs perfectly represented the boho style of Sienna Miller, Chloë Sevigny and Kate Bosworth and, in recent years, Gigi Hadid has been the face of the brand on the catwalk and in the Spring-Summer 2023 campaign.

So discover the story of one of fashion's most free-spirited design houses, from its avant-garde beginnings to its revolutionary journey under a series of superstar designers, and the reasons why it continues to inspire a dedicated following across the globe.

The Early
Years

The breezy, feminine Chloé woman

The bohemian spirit of Chloé was born from a woman who evoked everything that her fashion house stood for – independence, freedom and the essence of Parisian chic.

Gaby Aghion's name may have been eclipsed by Chloé's list of starry designers – Karl Lagerfeld, Stella McCartney, Clare Waight Keller, to name a few – but she was an incredibly inspiring entrepreneur; a woman who was ahead of her time in forging a fashion concept that became the go-to name for effortless style and feminine individuality. "She brought a spirit of challenge for women to empower themselves to be feminine that was important then, and is equally now," said Waight Keller when interviewed by *The New York Times* in 2014.

OPPOSITE In June 1958 the Spring/Summer 1959 Chloé collection was presented at the fashionable Brasserie Lipp in Paris.

Born Gabriella Hanoka in Alexandria, Egypt on 3 March 1921, she was the youngest of five children to well-to-do Jewish European parents. Her Greek father was the manager of a tobacco factory, and they moved in the elite circles of the Mediterranean port city, which has a long history as a thriving melting pot of different cultures and religions, and which attracted artistic visitors for its striking classical architecture.

She learned about fashion from her Italian mother, who would often ask her seamstress to recreate styles inspired by the latest designs from French magazines. The dark-haired, black-eyed Gaby, who haggled for silk and cotton in Alexandria's textile boutiques, was inventive in how she developed her own style. "Very quickly, I preferred what was a bit boyish," she said.

She first met her future husband, Raymond Aghion, at primary school when they were both just seven years old, and they married in 1940, at the age of nineteen. Raymond's parents, of Jewish-Italian origin, were from a family of bankers and cotton exporters, and he rebelled against this privilege with an interest in socialist politics. Alongside fellow left-wing intellectuals, he helped to form the Democratic Union in Egypt in 1939, becoming more and more involved when the Second World War broke out. Living under the weight of a global conflict, the young couple were socially conscious and actively involved in helping Yugoslavian refugees in Egypt. In 1945, with the declaration of peace, they made the decision to move to Paris, which turned out to be a prescient move: Egypt expelled its Jewish population in the 1950s.

In the year of their arrival, France was shattered from four years of occupation by Nazi Germany. However, following its liberation by Allied forces in 1944, post-war Paris was the epicentre of art and literature, and of intellectual and philosophical thought. The Left Bank, and in particular Saint-

OPPOSITE An early portrait of Chloé founder Gaby Aghion photographed by her husband Raymond Aghion.

Germain-des-Prés, also known as the Latin Quarter, was the bohemian heart of the city. It was a vibrant, youth-centred area where the zazou, existentialist and beatnik subcultures gathered at the tables and chairs outside Les Deux Magots, Café de Flore and Brasserie Lipp, or crowded into the smoky cave bars pulsating with jazz.

The affluent and modern Aghions moved in these artistic circles. Their close friends included writers Louis Aragon, Paul Eluard and Tristan Tzara; they spent time in the Left-Bank cafés with famous figures like Pablo Picasso and writer Lawrence Durrell. The intellectual bohemians were interested in social equality, and radical in thought, and it triggered in Gaby a need to create. Despite their comfortable lifestyle, which included holidays on the French Riviera, Gaby wanted to do more: "I wanted to have an activity of my own – not to make money, but because creating something of your own brings you great happiness and pride." With her friends' encouragement she realized fashion was the obvious choice, and in 1952 Gaby established her own business.

By the early 1950s the fashion industry in Paris was thriving. When he launched his New Look in 1947, Christian Dior had restored pride to a nation that had suffered so much following the Occupation. His ultra-feminine designs used excessive amounts of fabric, and in cinching and shaping a woman's body into that of an hourglass he dramatically switched the silhouette from wartime practicality to overt femininity. The international success of Dior was a triumph for Paris fashion as the city rose up again like Venus from the sea foam.

As well as Christian Dior, other prestigious couturiers included Jacques Fath and Pierre Balmain, Cristóbal Balenciaga and Hubert de Givenchy, who was the new kid in fashion when he established his house in 1952. Coco Chanel may have shuttered her business in 1939, but she made a spectacular comeback at the age of 71 in February 1954.

Through fashion, Paris cast a spell of enchantment, sprinkling magic dust over the ruins of the war, and creating an image of an artistic paradise, where every street corner featured a sophisticated Parisian girl against the backdrop of the Eiffel Tower, Montmartre and Notre Dame. But the reality of life in the city was quite different from what the fashion editorials would have people believe. Most people struggled with money, and couture from Paris's top salon was only attainable to the wealthiest women: those who travelled by chauffeur, and who possessed expense accounts. The alternative was to go to dressmakers, who didn't always create the cutting-edge look of the couture houses.

"You dressed in couture when you had the money," said Gaby, "and the rest of the time you wore clothes by what we called les couturières – dressmakers – because, after all, you needed a lot of clothes, morning, lunch, afternoon, evening." She said that the couturières copied the high fashion clothes, "but adding bits here and there and everything they added was horrible, so you ended up with this kind of half-baked couture."

Gaby understood that there was a gap in the market for high-quality fashion which was readily available to women who couldn't quite afford couture. She missed the skilled seamstresses of Alexandria, who tailored made-to-measure clothing as inspired by the designs in French fashion magazines. She remembered the young women in Egypt who wore light summer sport clothing, and who appeared much fresher and freer than the ordinary women on the streets of Paris.

Because she thought "women looked prettier on the beach than on the street", she wanted to recreate the simplicity of a minimalist silhouette as an alternative to the complexity of Dior, who was so extravagant and, she believed, out of touch. She grasped her opportunity to make a difference.

With her interest in left-wing politics, and a desire for equality, she wanted fashion to be more accessible. Her vision was to use good-quality fabrics to create feminine, nonrestrictive, alluring clothes that could be bought ready-made, with minimal alteration. She said: "A lot of things did not exist in France. Everything was yet to be invented, and this thrilled me."

Buying a quantity of cotton poplin fabric, she created six simple summer dresses, good quality and light enough for the sweltering city heat. These first dresses were easily alterable to fit, and were, she said, "very pretty, in poplin, a pale Oxford blue I like very much, midnight blue, berry pink, beige, black and white. I only had one shape – six colours – but everybody loved them!"

She packed them into a suitcase which she placed in the back of her car, and then drove around the city selling them to boutiques. As a welcome contrast to the stiff formality of haute couture, they sold out within days, and she ran up further designs. Rather than branding her dresses with her own name, as was the convention with fashion houses at the time, she chose to call her collection Chloé, after her close friend Chloé Huysmans. She thought the name was feminine, flirty and slightly audacious; she loved the appearance of the rounded letters, which she considered a perfect representation for her designs. At the time, boutiques were insistent on sewing their own label into clothes, "but I had the sass to request that the Chloé label remain," she said. The name, of Greek origin, meaning "young green shoot", is understood to represent fertility and the bloom of nature, and with Gaby's influence it would go hand in hand with the notion of feminine and fresh fashion.

Bohemian
Spirit

Fashion for the modern woman

Gaby Aghion was a visionary who designed her dresses for women to live and work in, at a time when there was an expectation that once married, they would stay at home. Her view of women as emancipated beings was counterintuitive to the prevailing view of the time.

She had pluck and drive, she was energetic and independent, and as a working woman with an independent outlook, she had a sense of the practical, as well as the poetic, in her designs. She hired former seamstresses from the recently closed Lucien Lelong salon, and turned the maid's room, or top-floor chambre de bonne, in her apartment into an atelier. She scoured for fabrics and buttons, and each day the seamstresses would cram themselves into the room as Gaby tried out different ideas. She jokingly described these early years as "hell", for the uncomfortable arrangements and sheer hard work required. Her cottage-industry fashion line was building a name for itself, and soon it would come to encapsulate a radical new mode of selling fashion.

After her initial success, Gaby teamed up with business partner Jacques Lenoir, and he was able to help move her burgeoning fashion house forward. She was incredibly focused and single-

OPPOSITE The Mirage black cocktail dress, for Autumn/Winter 1963, where the name of every piece began with an "M".

minded in her ambitions, despite some cynicism about her ready-to-wear business model. "I was carried away; it was like a tornado," she said. "I designed a small collection and decided to present it myself. I went to source the buttons, the fabrics. I was sticking my neck out. I was the client; I became the saleswoman. I encountered a lot of terrible disdain."

In 1956, Gaby's husband Raymond opened an art gallery which specialized in modern art, and that same year Gaby's son Philippe was born. As a very modern woman, she juggled with the demands of being a new mother while also launching a new fashion collection. But she was supported all the way by her husband. "I never saw my mother serving my father, ever," said her son. "That just wasn't how things were done at home. There was no machismo. They were equals. Both worked – both were emancipated."

Shortly after the birth of Philippe, she held her first prêt-à-porter fashion show in the suitably bohemian Café de Flore, situated at the intersection of the Boulevard Saint-Germain and the Rue Saint-Benoît. It was the cultural centre of the Left Bank, where artists, writers, philosophers and glamorous socialites would mix to create an intellectual, bohemian atmosphere. Jean-Paul Sartre and Simone de Beauvoir had gathered here to discuss their philosophy in the 1940s, and Juliette Gréco, the existentialist icon in her all black outfits, could be spotted there. Later in the 1950s, fashion was thrown into the mix. Models and designers, including Karl Lagerfeld, were often found at its tables, people-watching before design sessions and fittings in their ateliers. As Sartre once said: "The path to freedom begins at the Flore."

The café possessed exactly the right ethos for Chloé, a fashion house that was so different from the couture houses based on the gilded, sweeping boulevards of the chic 8th arrondissement. As would be a tradition for Chloé, the collection was shown in the

OPPOSITE A tweed skirt suit from the Autumn/Winter 196 collection, presente at the Parisian brasserie La Closeri des Lilas.

RIGHT The outdoor tables at the bustling Café de Flore in 1950 was a popular gathering place for writers, artists and fashion figures.

morning, while breakfast was being served and with models in their easy cocktail dresses sauntering between the tables. It was such a success that Gaby's twice-a-year shows became the highlight of the fashion calendar in Paris, as Chloé earned a reputation for sophisticated clothing with an off-beat Left Bank bent.

The Café de Flore wasn't the only Left Bank institution where Chloé was shown. The floral tiled walls of the Brasserie Lipp was the backdrop to one 1958 show, while a collection shown at the Belle Époque restaurant Closerie des Lilas was reviewed in *The New York Times* in December 1960. "The press sits around at tables drinking café au lait and munching croissants while the models weave in and out of the tables," the article described. Another quirk established with the Autumn/Winter 1958 llection was to use the same letter to name every item, beginning with "A". "Adorable" and "Amour" described the eces that season, including pretty dresses with full skirts and ws at the back. By Spring/Summer 1961, Chloé's ready-to-ear was connected to youth and joy in the press. With its eces all beginning with "F", one frilled wrap dress named the lou-flou" was hailed as a classic, and it came to define Gaby's eferred style – that of "le flou", or the light and fluid.

After being encouraged by Maïmé Arnodin, editor of *Jardin s Modes*, an influential French fashion magazine, Gaby stepped vay from being the sole creator. Instead, in 1958, Gaby opted bring in a team of designers to help with her collections, arking the beginning of Chloé as a home of encouragement r creatives. She had a unique eye for talent, and the first she red was Gérard Pipart, an avant-garde designer who had cut s teeth working for Jacques Fath, Hubert de Givenchy, and Marc Bohan at Jean Patou. In 1964 Pipart would leave Chloé to ork for Nina Ricci, where he was head designer for 35 years, ntil his retirement. Also joining the team was Christiane Bailly, ho had been a Balenciaga and Chanel model before a designer, d would later work in film costume; Graziella Fontana, an novative Italian designer who specialized in creating sharp nod" suits; and Maxime de La Falaise, an English model and cialite who married a French marquis and was a regular on e Paris social scene. Later additions to the team included Tan iudicelli and Michèle Rosier, nicknamed the "Vinyl Girl" for er use of vinyl in fashion; both were part of the Paris ready-to-ear movement of the 1960s, known as "Le Style". Rosier spoke Eugenia Sheppard of the *Herald Tribune* in February 1965 bout her love for designing dresses for Chloé. In choosing to ne the pleats of a mauve dress with vibrant contrasting shades, e described herself as a "multicolour girl".

A two-room apartment on rue de Miromesnil then served as Gaby's headquarters, with the office space in one room and the workroom filled with sketches and reams of fabric in the other. They moved at the end of the 1960s to a grand Haussmannian apartment on Place Saint-Philippe-du-Roule. The designers would present their sketches to Gaby individually, and she would then choose which ones would make it into the collection.

The Autumn/Winter 1961 collection offered wearable pieces for the modern woman which combined the masculine and feminine, such as a tartan cape suit, worn with a shirt and tie, button-down wool dresses and pussy-bow blouses. For the Spring/Summer 1962 collection, shown at the Hôtel du Palais d'Orsay, there were daring backless dresses, and sheer gowns with frills and satin bows. Again, with their transparency and sensuality they reflected the easy style of Chloé.

Gaby was fully involved in the business, not just with overseeing the bohemian dresses and tailored suits, but with her strategy for distribution and advertising, and building close relationships with department stores. Affectionate and animated, but also incredibly focused, she created a fashion house that spoke to women for its mix of timeless femininity and tomboy sass.

By the mid-1960s Parisian culture was focused on youth and celebrity. This exciting decade was marked by a novel explosion of expression, and the new wave of forward-thinking designers included Yves Saint Laurent, Pierre Cardin and André Courrèges. Their focus turned to ready-to-wear, with Saint Laurent launching his own Left Bank-inspired line, Rive Gauche. While being in the right position to capture the youthful zeitgeist, Chloé's luxury fashions would be further reinvigorated by a ground-breaking designer who possessed endless energy and vision.

OPPOSITE Models wearing Totem and Totem Bis, dresses from the Spring/Summer 1966 collection. The dresses are in black wool crepe decorated with a series of rectangle in shades of yellow pink, orange, white and sky blue.

Karl
Lagerfeld

The chic fashion house for the boho Jet Set

A regular customer at the Café de Flore was Karl Lagerfeld, a young and eccentric German who was finding his way in the rarefied fashion world of Paris. For Karl, the café was not just his favourite hang-out spot in St Germain, but it was the centre of life. Arriving each morning in an open-top Mercedes, he made a dramatic entrance in high-heeled boots and a floor-length fur coat, and then positioned himself at one of the tables as he pored over the latest issue of *Vogue*.

Karl Otto Lagerfeld was born in Hamburg, Germany in September 1933. His mother was a former lingerie saleswoman and his father was managing director of Glücksklee, which manufactured condensed milk. From a young age Karl had an artistic mind, visiting museums and always sketching, even when in his school classroom, and from his provincial, bourgeois life, Karl dreamed of Paris. When Christian Dior brought a fashion show to Hamburg, displaying his New Look, Karl knew that this would be his future, and he announced to his parents: "I am leaving to become a fashion designer in Paris."

OPPOSITE Karl Lagerfeld with Chloé models wearing the Autumn/Winter 1976 collection, outside the the Chloé boutique, which had just moved from 50 rue du Bac to 3 rue de Gribeauval.

ABOVE Karl Lagerfeld at work in the studio with Gaby Aghion (seated) in 1972.

OPPOSITE A jersey evening gown from the Autumn/Winter 1973 collection was inspired by the glitz of Paris's nightlife.

When he first arrived in the city as an ambitious 19-year-old in 1952 (the same year Gaby Aghion was launching her fashion house), he went straight to the Left Bank, moving into a hotel on the Rue de la Sorbonne. There he lived like a character in one of his favourite films, 1951's *Sous le ciel de Paris* (*Under the Paris Sky*), which featured a fashion show in front of the Eiffel Tower.

In 1954 Karl entered a prestigious design contest sponsored by the International Wool Secretariat. He was selected from 6,000 entries as one of the winners for his design for a yellow calf-length coat with a V-neck at the back, while another ambitious up-and-coming designer, Yves Saint Laurent, won for his dress design. As part of the prize, Karl's sketch was brought to life by the couturier Pierre Balmain, who then offered Karl a job at his label, which had been established in 1945 and was known for its sophisticated, elegant designs beloved by celebrities and socialites.

Karl spent four years working as an assistant for this prestigious couturier, with the Balmain atelier located in "the Triangle d'Or", the luxury fashion quarters centred around

POSITE Geometric
sey and flannel
its were part of
e Autumn/Winter
73 collection.

LOW The Tertulia
nidress with its
nd-painted silk
is designed by Karl
gerfeld for Spring/
mmer 1966.

the Champs-Élysées and the Avenue George V. Then in 1958 he was named as artistic director for Jean Patou, an almost vintage design house beloved for its best-selling perfume, Joy, whose founder had died 20 years before. Despite the prestigious position, he felt stifled by the staid atmosphere, and with only two collections a year he needed to be kept busier. "Tradition is a good thing, but it must remain alive," he said. "You have to inject some life into it or it just becomes a respectable habit, something negative."

Karl hadn't made much impact during his tenure, so in January 1963 he left Patou by mutual agreement to work as a freelance ready-to-wear designer for brands including Mario Valentino and Monoprix. To move from haute couture to ready-to-wear was a gamble because it was considered less prestigious, but he also understood that society was on the cusp of change, and that the future lay in a more democratic fashion.

He was aware of Chloé and Gaby Aghion's unique model of hiring a team of designers to bring a constant stream of fresh ideas to her two collections each year. In 1963 he arrived for a meeting with Gaby armed with a series of sketches. As she flicked through them, she lingered over "a rather charming dress in beige shantung which Karl had drawn with the most ravishing yellow tights. No one thought about doing tights with the outfit at that time." Her business partner, Jacques Lenoir, was also impressed, and they agreed to hire Karl and add him to their team.

From the moment he brought his ideas to the table, it was clear that Karl's talents were extraordinary. Like Gaby, he was fascinated by youth culture and street style, and he would explore the Left Bank, observing what the students at the Sorbonne were wearing, sketching their styles, and then translating it into designs for Chloé. In January 1964 a fashion reporter, Nathalie Pernikoff, described how it was "chic to be off-beat in Paris", adding that Chloé "is considered by fashion experts to be one of the most exciting in Paris". The team created "an enchanting collection of beautifully made clothes," she went on to say, which featured "white or yellow lisle stockings and low heeled dress shoes", just like Lagerfeld's initial sketch.

Gaby was a mentor and supporter of Karl, and she encouraged him to tone down his tendency for the baroque, in

OPPOSITE Lagerfeld's geometric prints, influenced by the art deco interior designer Armand-Albert Rateau, featured in the Spring/Summer 1973 catwalk show Restaurant Lauren

OPPOSITE The
Spring/Summer
1974 collection by
Karl Lagerfeld was
shown in a 200-piece
runway presentation
two hours long in
restaurant Laurent.

RIGHT Baltique, an
ivory crepe de Chine
poncho dress hand-
painted with black
and water green art
deco motifs and its
matching parasol
from the Spring/
Summer 1974
collection.

favour of fresher, less fussy clothing. "I have always said fashion should be as fresh as a salad," she said. "There would be designs among the sketches that I set aside as right, other sketches that I would put in a different pile. Karl would want to rip up the sketches in the second pile straight away and I would say, 'Wait, don't throw them out. We'll keep them to the side for the moment. It's not exactly right for now, but there is an idea there.'"

Karl contributed two designs to the Autumn/Winter 1964 collection, as Gaby already had three other designers working on this collection (Graziella Fontana, Michèle Rosier and Tan Giudicelli). She tested him with more than ten models for Spring/Summer 1965, and soon he was producing more and more for Chloé, while balancing his other assignments, including for Fendi. As well as studying the contemporary style of students, Lagerfeld had a voracious appetite for art and design history, particularly art deco at the beginning of the 1970s and eighteenth-century baroque and the end of this decade, and these influences were woven into his collections. A major art deco exhibition was held at the Musée des Arts décoratifs in Paris in 1966, and this sparked a revival of the streamlined style with its bold geometric prints.

One of Karl's most famous designs was the dynamic Tertulia dress for Spring/Summer 1966, which featured hand-painted art nouveau motifs. It was representative of the unstructured, whimsical style of Chloé, and captured the same carefree vibe as the Pucci psychedelic prints and Ossie Clark and Celia Birtwell designs, as favoured by the hippie jet set. The Chloé girl was young and free, with a bohemian ethos, and perfectly in tune with the look of the late 1960s youthquake era – that of loose, transparent gowns printed with vibrant patterns. In 1969 Jane Birkin was photographed by Guy Bourdin for

Vogue Paris, wearing Chloé's high-necked draped minidresses and a white asymmetrical jumpsuit in silk jersey from the Spring/Summer 1969 collection. Icon Birkin wearing Chloé encapsulated the countercultural mood of the time, where the hippie-era came to a head with Woodstock, and reflected how Karl was completely in tune with youth culture.

A series of Chloé high, ruffled necklines and billowing sleeves were also incredibly popular, appearing in British *Vogue* in 1967, which praised them as "the essence of the dandy", and his hand-painted dresses were also generating much attention. "Karl's designs for Chloé were simply sublime," said his close friend and editor of *Interview* magazine, Sandra Brant. "It was when we were all madly collecting Art Deco and the fabrics and style of Chloé were very influenced by that. I still have all my old Chloé from that period and the designs are fantastic – filled with wit and humor."

As Karl excelled, the other designers began to leave, or were chased away by the threat of his talents. Tan Giudicelli would start his own collection and launch a series of perfumes, Maxime de La Falaise moved to New York, and in 1975 he was named exclusive designer with the launch of the Chloé perfume. As Karl would later say: "I sold more than them. Perhaps I also got rid of them."

In May 1968 riots broke out in the Latin Quarter, around the streets of the Sorbonne. They were led by students, who fiercely protested inequality and railed against the bourgeoisie, and the disruption coincided with a change in fashion. That same month Cristóbal Balenciaga retired and closed down his house. Coco Chanel, the grand dame of haute couture, died in 1971. The young and bohemian crowd preferred to pick things from a boutique rather than spend hours in fittings, and many of Paris's traditional couture houses closed the doors. This shift in how

OPPOSITE The preview for Spring Summer 1974, on the streets of Paris showcasing Marlene Dietrich-style glamour.

OPPOSITE A dress with belt and sash detailing from the Autumn/Winter 1974 collection by Karl Lagerfeld at Palais de Chaillot.

RIGHT The Spring/ Summer 1975 presentation at Palais de Chaillot had a bucolic feel, and included this simply chic outfit with its tissue-thin suede coat dyed in a shade evocative of eighteenth-century watercolours, accessorized with a shepherd's crook.

fashion was being consumed ensured Chloé was at the cutting edge, and with Karl as lead designer.

He was tireless in his output, managing his fur collections for Fendi while also being the driving force for Chloé throughout the 1970s and becoming increasingly famous through his contributions to the fashion house's collections. His knitwear, pop art print dresses, silk scarves, accessories and romantic lingerie tea gowns were eternally popular. "Women fought for those dresses," said Gaby. "I got calls from all over the world."

In 1972 Jeannette Alfandari teamed up with Gaby and Jacques Lenoir to open the first Chloé boutique in Paris, at 50 rue du Bac, and this new space was instrumental in helping move the maison forward commercially. Chloé was now being worn by some of the most famous celebrities in the world – Maria Callas, Brigitte Bardot, Grace Kelly and Jackie Kennedy. Chloé was given a further stamp of approval when Grace Mirabella, the editor-in-chief of *Vogue*, who replaced Diana Vreeland in 1971, chose to wear a Chloé white turtleneck studded with pearls to her wedding rather than selecting Yves Saint Laurent.

One of Karl's muses was Princess Caroline of Monaco, the wild child daughter of Grace Kelly who was seen in Paris's nightclubs in Chloé. Another favourite was Paloma Picasso, daughter of the artist, who in the summer of 1973 was photographed by Helmut Newton in Karl's Saint-Tropez apartment, wearing a figure-hugging black dress by Chloé, with gold bracelets and cuffs on her wrist and one breast exposed. The hedonism of Paris in the 1970s was captured in images by Newton and Guy Bourdin, who revealed the decadence and freedom of the era in their fashion photography for *Vogue Paris* which very often featured Chloé garments.

OSITE Pat
veland wearing
élie, an off-the-
ulder long dress
inkish-beige
printed with
e flowers, at the
ng/Summer 1975
ection, which
an ode to Marie
oinette with its
nantic, pastoral
e.

LEFT The preview
the Spring/Summ
1975 collection, w
easy separates or
the streets of Par

OPPOSITE The
Autumn/Winter 1
collection at Palai
des Congrès, whi
was Karl Lagerfel
official first as
sole designer, was
praised for its ligh
layerings of crêpe
Chine silk garmen
and references a
mix of Eastern an
Western influenc

André Leon Talley would describe in his memoir, *The Chiffon Trenches*, that Karl's surreal touches, such as plastic tulips on a necklace, or robot prints, were "youthful and inspired", and that even the way he organized his runway was different. He didn't assign his models a specific costume, rather they could choose what they wished to wear from the rack. And as a thank you, he would allow them to keep those items afterwards.

The models that Karl used on the catwalk were also the faces of the Paris cultural scene, including the Americans Pat Cleveland, Donna Jordan and Jerry Hall. They were inspired by the glamour of the classic Hollywood icons like Marlene Dietrich, posing and dancing on the catwalk, and holding their bodies with a certain attitude. Pat Cleveland recalled how she and Donna Jordan would not only model for Chloé, but would wear the lightweight dresses and chic coats when touring the city's cafés and nightclubs.

Karl was a mysterious and unique figure in Paris, with his signature ponytail and his sunglasses. He would spend his evenings at the gay hotspots of Paris with a crew of avant-garde, uber-fashionable figures, such as fashion illustrator Antonio Lopez and art director Juan Ramos, who arrived from New York to sketch Chloé for *Elle* magazine. Seamstress Anita Briey entered into the city's fashion world when she was hired by Chanel in 1955, and at the end of 1966 she switched to Chloé, working as the "seconde d'atelier" with Karl. She remembered, "he was pretty eccentric, arriving in his convertible with a honk of a horn. He would stop by Dalloyau, an excellent bakery on the corner, to buy pastries for everyone in the atelier."

The Autumn/Winter 1973 Chloé collection was shown in April of that year at Restaurant Laurent on the Champs-Élysées. Dresses were sleek and glitzy – draped jersey dresses and glittering beaded jackets – and were reflective of the burgeoning disco movement and Karl's own extracurricular activities at Le Sept nightclub.

OPPOSITE Texan model Jerry Hall walking the catwa[l]k for the Autumn/Winter 1976 collection wearing Donna Anna, a gold lamé dress embroidered with gold lace bands, overlaid with a bla[ck] chiffon dress.

OPPOSITE The
rear view of the
Autumn/Winter 1977
collection by Karl
Lagerfeld included
Chantomas, this
elaborately draped
piece in black flannel,
and slouchy boots.

RIGHT The Autumn/
Winter 1977
collection referenced
the eighteenth-
century fop, with
romantic, billowing
blouses in Chantilly
lace.

"There was a time, in the 1970s, when I hated to be out of town for more than 24 hours. There was the feeling that, wherever you were in Europe, you did whatever you had to do to make it back to Paris for drinks at the Café de Flore and dancing at Le Sept," he said.

As well as disco, his designs in the early 1970s represented Old Hollywood, with tailored wide-legged trousers which wouldn't look out of place on a 1930s Katharine Hepburn, trailing gowns with pleated skirts, and trench coats with long leather boots, as seen on the Autumn/Winter 1974 catwalk.

In 1975 Karl Lagerfeld signed a perfume deal with Gaby Aghion, Jacques Lenoir and Elizabeth Arden, and he received a profit share under a new company, Karl Lagerfeld Productions. The Chloé perfume was launched with a tour of America, and in New York he met André Leon Talley, a friend of Andy Warhol, who profiled him for *Interview* magazine. "Karl Lagerfeld, the genius, who pours silk over the body with the same distinction as he poured his new fragrance – Chloé – on America," praised the writer, in awe of the designer.

Throughout the 1970s Karl continued to create floaty, free-spirited styles without linings or hems, which served to create a sense of freedom from structure. From his art deco influence, he moved on to French eighteenth-century designs, with references to the Marie Antoinette shepherdess and milkmaid-inspired dresses in the Spring/Summer 1975 collection. The Chloé Spring/Summer 1975 collection was praised for the ruffled blouses, frilled dresses with aprons and straw hats, shawls and flower corsages, which were an antithesis of the disco look. The *Chicago Tribune* in November 1974 described how this collection had "put Paris back on the throne of world fashion leadership" and praised the "unlined poplin duster coats" and a group of tissue-thin suede coats dyed in shades evocative of eighteenth-century watercolors.

OPPOSITE Chloé's Spring/Summer 1978 collection was an exercise in subdued pastels to fit with the economic uncertainty of the times.

The accessories in his collections for Chloé were typically avant-garde and eye-catching. Swimming costumes featured belts made from plastic bubbles; there were flying-saucer hats with crêpe-de-Chine disco skirts, a live parrot on a shoulder, and silk fans. He also teamed dresses with tennis shoes – which, at that time, was unheard of.

Talley said: "The Chloé shows were way ahead of everything. They were the avant-garde, yet they were sophisticated and raffiné. I would go to the showroom and meet with the owner, Gaby Aghion – Karl had a great relationship with her. It was a small company but it was full of wonderful wonders – the clothes were just exquisite. The clothes were new and the way he showed the clothes was new. His runway shows were always exciting."

As well as the pastoral look of fresh cotton and lace, Karl also referenced the flamboyance of the New Romantics, which embraced foppish masculine styles. This would influence a shift towards a sharper image for the 1980s.

Karl believed in the inclusion of wit in fashion, and when he was interviewed by Bill Boggs in New York in 1979 he said: "Fashion without humour is a bore." Among the gowns he showed to the audience were a navy blue satin dress with a light bulb embroidered on the front, and a high-necked puffed-sleeve gown with sequin motifs of perfume bottles.

One of the most iconic Lagerfeld designs was the "Angkor" violin dress for Spring/Summer 1983, which was in sync with the musical theme of that collection – there were also piano handbags and belts, and dresses branded with glittering guitars, which emphasized the music theme. The violin dresses would be brought back to life when worn by Chloë Sevigny in 2013, and with reproductions worn by both Olivia Wilde and Margaret Zhang at the 2023 Met Gala, in tribute to Karl.

His Autumn/Winter 1983 collection featured a plethora of workmen's tools and hardware, including collars and shoulders

OPPOSITE Gladys, dress from the Spring/Summer 1978 collection that is all creamy lace and translucent chiffon.

LEFT The Autumn/
Winter 1978
collection was rich
and expressive,
with designs in tur
with the emerging
New Romantic
movement, includ
this dress named
Internat.

OPPOSITE In the
Spring/Summer
1979 collection,
Lagerfeld chose to
highlight the waist
for form-fitting
1940s Hollywood-
inspired silhouette
featuring a tongue
in-cheek flying
saucer print for
this dress named
Libation.

magnificently embroidered with jewelled wrenches, hammers and pliers, taps dripping with pearls, and evening dresses with shower heads spraying sparkling rhinestone beads. When it was shown at a benefit show at Radio City Music Hall, Gaby Aghion and Jacques Lenoir were in the audience to welcome the applause.

Karl's contract with Chloé was due to expire at the end of 1983, and he was approached by Alain Wertheimer, the owner of Chanel, to sign a lucrative deal to design their couture line. There were questions as to whether he would continue to work for Chloé at the same time, particularly as there were rumours of a rift with Gaby Aghion.

Ultimately, Karl's farewell show for Chloé was the Spring/Summer 1984 collection, held in October 1983. It was a pointed tribute to dressmaking, with witty references to fashion history including sleek Grecian silhouettes with embroidered trompe

OPPOSITE Adagio, cocktail dress, embroidered with rows of clear single beads, crystals and an electric guitar motif in white, black, and red sequins. From the music-inspired Spring/Summer 1983 collection.

RIGHT Models Farida Bayle wearing Bain and Suzanne DeWitt Sunrise, dresses embroidered with shower showerhead and water-jet motifs in sequins, single beads and silver rhinestones from the Autumn/Winter 1983 collection.

l'oeil of wrapped clothes, and motifs of spools of thread, bobbin thimbles and open scissors. The backdrop to the catwalk feature an illustration with a plane in the sky, pulling a banner emblazo with the Chloé logo and flown by a pilot with a ponytail, clearly Karl, which hinted that he was moving on to new horizons.

Gaby described the split as "difficult", particularly as their relationship had been increasingly fraught over the previous few years. "If I wasn't there for the fittings, he held it against me. I was very busy at the time, too. And so there was a kind of small separation even then between us," she later said.

While Karl launched his own ready-to-wear label under his own name, Gaby selected French designer Guy Paulin to be his successor, with the aim that he would continue to make the elegant, feminine clothes that were associated with Chloé. But there were fears that the magic Karl brought to the maison was now lost. Karl's legacy for Chloé had been extraordinary. "At the house of Chloé, Lagerfeld invented the concept of prêt-à-porter de luxe, which put Paris ready-to-wear fashion on track," said Su Menkes in *The Times* in 1986.

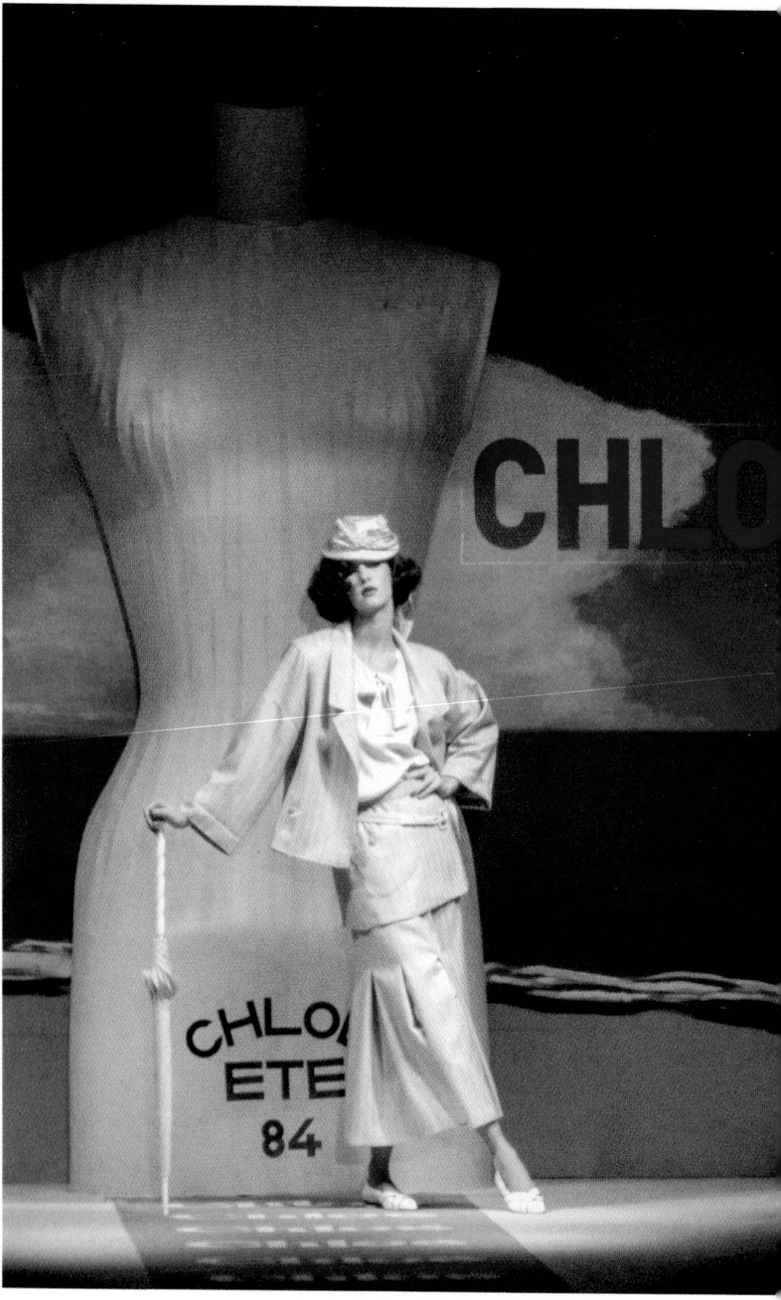
CHLO
CHLO
ETE
84

OPPOSITE
Campanule suit
with midi-length
skirt from the
Spring/Summer
1984 presentation
in the "Salle Sully"
in the Palais du
Louvre.

RIGHT The Spring/
Summer 1984
collection included
cintre, a whimsical
dress embellished
with a dress on a
hanger, or cintre in
French.

Supermodel Luxury

32
26

53
2,5

Chlo

A fresh perspective and a new approach

When Karl Lagerfeld revealed that he was breaking away from Chloé after a 20-year collaboration, there was much anticipation as to the new direction of its ready-to-wear. But when the Autumn/ Winter 1984 collection by designer Guy Paulin was unveiled, it was ultimately a disappointment or, in the words of Bernadine Morris of *The New York Times*, an "unmitigated disaster". His slouchy skirts and loose sweaters were not well received by the press or by buyers, who were expecting to see the elegant and humorous evening gowns that Lagerfeld had specialized in.

P aulin, originally from the Champagne region of France, worked his way up from elevator boy at the Paris Printemps department store and into their design team. After stints as a designer for a number of labels including Mary Quant and Max Mara, he founded his own ready-to-wear label, shortly before being offered the top job at Chloé. He may have described the appointment as a dream, but the reviews were devastating, with *Women's Wear Daily* (*WWD*) dismissing his designs as "unfocused and undirected, notable only in its penchant for Fifties bargain-basement looks and a muddy color palette that appeals to Middle Europe, but not to Middle America."

OPPOSITE The Autumn/Winter 1984 collection, presented at the "Salle Sully" at the Palais du Louvre, was noted for its muted palette.

Two weeks after the Paris showings, Gaby hired the French designer Philippe Guibourgé to create evening wear for the Spring/Summer 1985 collection, which would work alongside Paulin's simpler sporty dresses and chemises. "I thought Philip would be better for the kind of dresses the customers are asking for," she said.

Philippe Guibourgé was a former designer for Jacques Fath and Christian Dior, and had launched the house of Chanel's ready-to-wear collection in 1977 to great fanfare. He specialize in the dramatic, with silk and rayon jersey in rich colours such as royal purple, navy and red, and with details such as draping the hip, embroidery and beading.

For the Autumn/Winter 1985 collection, Gaby reintroduce her preferred mode of working with a team of designers, including Irish designer Peter O'Brien, who had trained at Central Saint Martins College of Art in London and Parsons

School of Design in New York, and Italian Luciano Soprani. "We don't want just one star designer," she said, perhaps in a pointed reference to Karl Lagerfeld. It was no surprise Guy Paulin announced he would be leaving Chloé to return to his own label, and in 1985 Gaby made the decision to sell Chloé to Alfred Dunhill Ltd (now under Richemont), although she continued to keep close ties.

In October of that year, this new management chose to revamp Chloé by featuring that one star designer – Peter O'Brien, who was 34 at the time. The maison had received lacklustre reviews over the previous few years, and it was thought that this new approach could be a welcome change. His debut solo collection for Spring/Summer 1986 was well received for his use of primary colours and humorous patterns, including a black tiered gown featuring embroidered croquet symbols. The *Daily Telegraph* wrote that he introduced "a sense of wit and humour it is hoped will assert a new, young contemporary image for the house, which has sadly missed the talent of Karl Lagerfeld."

Peter O'Brien's collection for Autumn/Winter 1986 was more severe, with a prim school teacher feel of grey pleated skirts and long flannel coats. It would be his last collection, and stepping into his place in August 1986 was Carlos Rodriguez, who came from the Italian brand Maska. His Spring/Summer 1987 collection was considered confusing, with a predominant black and white palette, conservative ecclesiastical coats and hats, round sunglasses and a white lace bustier dress. With Chloé still failing to make an impact post-Karl, a shake-up was needed.

In 1987 the young, edgy French designer Martine Sitbon was appointed, with the hopes she could return Chloé to being the must-have fashion house for cool young things. Like Gaby, Martine was originally from North Africa. Born in Casablanca, she moved to Paris as a child, and with an interest in shopping in flea markets and fusing fashion with music, she studied at

OSITE The
ng/Summer
7 show included
croquet-
bellished tiered
ss, modelled by
pessa Hennink.

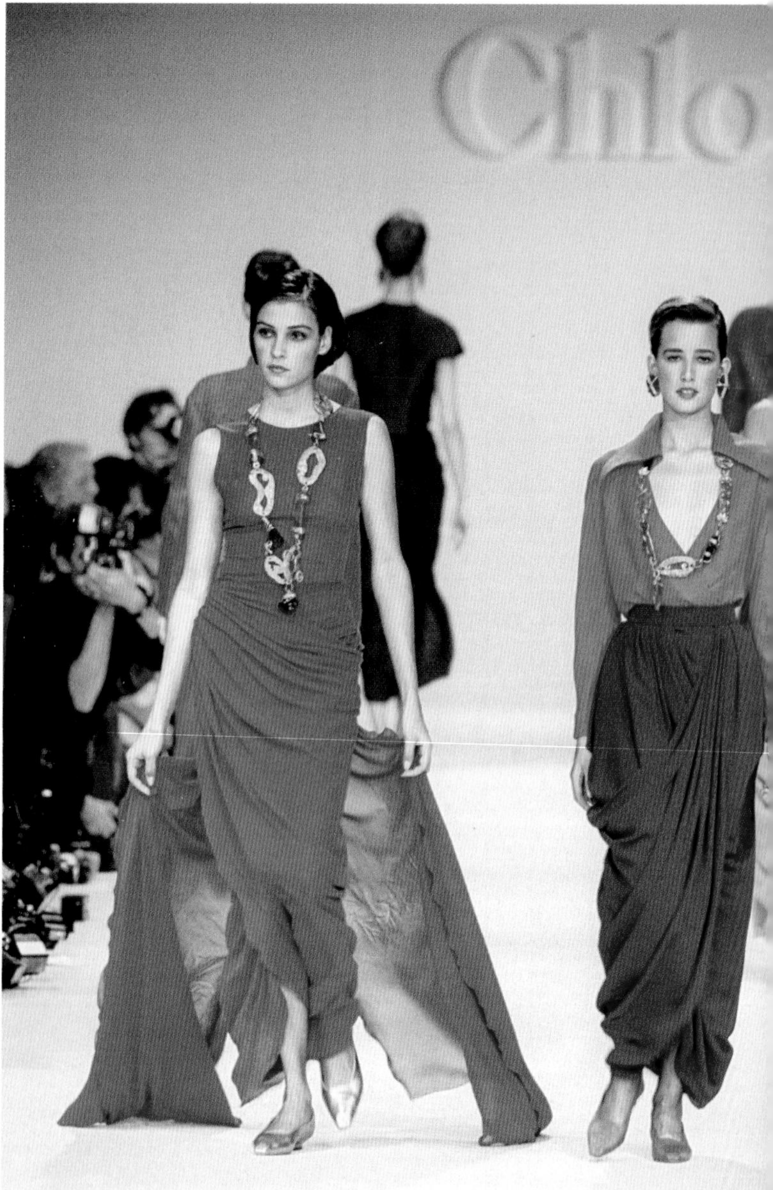

the Paris fashion institute Studio Berçot, graduating in 1974. She worked as a freelance designer, until founding her own Martine Sitbon line in 1986. *Vogue* named her as a talent to watch because she had "a certain charm – an insouciance – and a somewhat younger Paris-made way to dress."

She continued with her eponymous line, while also breathing new life into Chloé. As the first creative director since Karl, Martine brought a fresh perspective and a hip edge with her sophisticated but rebellious designs touching upon the 1970s silhouette, something that other designers weren't doing at the time. She admired musicians like David Bowie, and the subcultures of the 1960s and 1970s, including folk, glam rock and the Hell's Angels. She combined these influences with the breezy femininity of the traditional Chloé woman, and a sense of nostalgia with touches of Victoriana, Old Hollywood and good tailoring. Her debut Spring/Summer 1988 collection used a muted palette of rust, taupe and aubergine, with taffeta gowns, straw hats and quirky patterns, which she referred to as a "Parisian touch".

Following her Autumn/Winter 1989 collection, the press were taking note of Sitbon's designs for Chloé, and American buyers were once again snapping up the soft-tailored suits, peasant blouses and waistcoats, and embroidered jackets with a Mandarin influence. One fashion critic described it as having "something for everyone: hot pants, gold bell-bottom jumpsuits, tail coats and Russian peasant outfits, complete with boots and saber belts. Despite her infatuation with ethnic looks and 1960s reruns she showed superb shawl-collared coats, snug jackets and flowing pants in speckled tweed and slinky black tuxedos."

Sitbon's Spring/Summer 1990 collection featured polka dots, knotted skirts and loose checked pants, which were described as being perfect for a trip to Deauville in the 1930s. To ensure Chloé was reflecting the zeitgeist, she hired the new supermodels

OPPOSITE Yasmen Ghauri modelling a polka-dot silk dress from Martine Sitbon's Spring/ Summer 1990 collection.

LEFT Linda
Evangelista
modelling a
spectacular bead
off-white minidre
for the Spring/
Summer 1991
presentation in
Paris.

Helena Christensen, Naomi Campbell and Yasmeen Ghauri to walk the catwalk and to appear in advertising campaigns. In *Vogue*, Linda Evangelista was styled as Ava Gardner in a silver gown from the Autumn/Winter 1990 collection, which also featured shimmering hooded and gothic dresses.

When Mounir Moufarrige was named as the new president of Chloé, he announced a younger, more feminine approach. In response Sitbon's next collections burst with colour. For the Autumn/Winter 1991 showing, there were ribbed sky blue jumpsuits worn with contrasting tomato red coats, a vibrant floral print coat and jewel-encrusted cocktail dresses. Her Spring/Summer 1992 collection was similarly bold and fun, with pop-art prints, flouncing lilac and lemon blouses and sparkling minidresses. The accessories were also a hit, with Selfridges devoting a section in their store to the Parisian silk scarves, leather bags and colourful jewellery.

Despite the gradual impact she had made in her nine seasons, Martine Sitbon's tenure at Chloé came to an end in 1992 – and Karl Lagerfeld made a fanfare of a return. In the 1990s there was a dramatic shift in the way the fashion industry operated, with big conglomerates now controlling the industry. In 1992 Dunhill Holdings bought Karl's eponymous brand, and as part of this deal, it was negotiated for him to make his long-awaited return to Chloé.

At Paris Fashion Week in October 1992, everyone was talking about Karl's Spring/Summer 1993 collection – anticipating which direction he would be going in. With a theme likened to Monet's garden, and with a catwalk featuring a painted backdrop of a cloudy and star-studded sky and cherubs, the world's top models, including Naomi Campbell with flowers and butterflies in her afro-style hair, paraded a soft, bohemian and ultra-feminine collection in pastel colours. It played into the phenomenon of grunge and the new dressed-down subcultures,

OPPOSITE Veronica
Webb in classic
pastels, muted
neutrals and tan
colours on the
runway for Spring/
Summer 1993.

RIGHT Naomi
Campbell as a
bohemian queen,
with flowers and
butterflies in her
hair, for Spring/
Summer 1993.

with Suzy Menkes writing in *Vogue*: "Lagerfeld's Chloé dresses are a hippie revival that expresses a new freedom, softness, and tenderness for women in the 1990s."

Karl was once again tireless in his productivity, running ten major collections each year for Fendi, Chanel, Lagerfeld and Chloé, where he was assisted by Virginie Viard, imported by him from Chanel. His shows would also feature the supermodels, who brought glamour and Amazonian beauty to the catwalk. He continued with the 1970s vibe at Chloé for future collections, with trailing boho frocks and wool dresses with long boots, and his Spring/Summer 1994 output was decidedly neoclassical. With Kate Moss in an Empire line printed minidress and headband, Claudia Schiffer in a pale belted tunic, and Nadja Auermann barefoot and in a white midriff-revealing top and flowing skirt, *WWD* described it as "Karl's Toga Party". Autumn/Winter 1994 was a tribute to the Snow Queen, with richer colours, fur edgings and icy crowns, and the next romantically feminine collections played into the mid-1990s trend for candy-coloured sweaters and skirts, delicate lace and lingerie detail.

By 1997 there were rumours that Karl Lagerfeld was once again planning to part ways with Chloé, and indeed Autumn/Winter 1997 would turn out to be his last season. This collection was a celestial space odyssey, as models with vibrant-coloured stripes in their hair walked in front of a planetary backdrop, wearing knitted dresses and evening gowns that appeared as if sprinkled with moon dust.

Following months of gossip as to who would replace him, in May 1997 Chloé made headlines again when it was announced the successor was a young woman with a rock pedigree. "He's been abandoned by Chloé for a younger woman," said *The New York Times*, on news that 25-year-old Stella McCartney had been appointed as creative director, welcoming in a new era.

OPPOSITE Karl Lagerfeld's final collection for Autumn/Winter 1997 was a space exploration of the romantic and the celestial.

Stella's Time
to Shine

The British are here to stay

When Stella McCartney revealed her debut collection for
Chloé during Paris Fashion Week in October 1997, the Opera
House's gilded salon was filled with a who's who of British
popular culture. On the runway were Kate Moss, Alek Wek
and Jodie Kidd, and in the audience were Stella's parents,
Paul and Linda McCartney, Paul's Beatles' bandmate Ringo
Star, David Bailey, the "It" photographer of the Swinging
Sixties, and Gaby Aghion, the first lady of Chloé.

Following her appointment, the relatively inexperienced
McCartney immediately brought a British sensibility to
the French brand, perfectly fusing the mid-1990s Cool
Britannia phenomenon with Parisian boho chic.

As the soundtrack to this first show blasted out 'Ain't it Sweet',
she revealed soft, feminine designs juxtaposed with masculine
tailoring. There were pale, barely there slip dresses, lace-trimmed
camisoles, white cotton blouses and skirts, and wide-legged
trouser suits, all touched with an effortless rock 'n' roll attitude
that harked back to the Chloé of the 1970s.

OPPOSITE Stella McCartney with Kate Moss, celebrating the
finale of her debut Spring/Summer 1998 show.

The Times hailed her collection with the headline "The British are Here to Stay", placing her name alongside Alexander McQueen at Givenchy and John Galliano at Christian Dior as British designers now heading up French design houses. One person who had not been so happy about her appointment was Karl Lagerfeld, who, with his usual acerbic wit, referred to her as the "Baby Beatle", and said: "I thought they would choose a big name. They did, but in music, not fashion."

By the time Stella was named creative director at the beginning of 1997, Chloé had lost the lustre that had attracted so many bright young things, and even Lagerfeld's much heralded return in 1992 had failed to provide the required oomph. As the *Philadelphia Inquirer* wrote in 1998: "Chloé and upscale stores such as Bergdorf are wishing on this star, hoping that she can spread enough stardust around to return the house to glory."

Stella's parents had been figureheads of the hippie era of the 1970s with their band Wings, and Linda McCartney had owned a number of Chloé pieces from that time, keeping them in a trunk, perhaps with the thought of passing them on to her daughters.

"What's funny about Chloé is I grew up knowing it on that level," Stella said in April 1997. "Friends of my parents have called and have been so over the moon and proud because when they were growing up it was a hot label. My generation has no idea of that. It's not doing that at the moment."

As a student at Central Saint Martins, Stella tried to keep her head down and blend in so that she could be judged on her work rather than who her parents were. She compulsively scoured flea markets to source Victorian glass buttons and Edwardian lace for her degree collection, and as an extra boost to her studies, she apprenticed with a tailor on Savile Row. Yet her graduation show in 1995 was anything but quiet. She

OPPOSITE Naomi Campbell modelli[n]g a satin and lace slip for the Spring Summer 1998 sho[w]

LEFT Stella
McCartney's
Autumn/Winter
1998 collection
revealed her love
of combining
sharp tailoring
with sleek satin.

asked her friends Kate Moss, Yasmin Le Bon and Naomi Campbell to model for her, and in the front row were her proud parents, alongside Twiggy, the model who defined 1960s London.

After graduation she employed two part-time assistants to help her launch her own label, which she sold from her basement flat in Notting Hill. These first collections were an edgy combination of Savile Row tailoring and lace-trimmed slip dresses that would become her signature, but it was proving more stressful for the novice designer than she had imagined. "I just hadn't envisaged how difficult or expensive sourcing fabrics and putting out a range could be. I was juggling everything, doing everything the wrong way around. I couldn't sleep at night for worrying."

The president of Chloé, Mounir Moufarrige, was after a designer who could reach younger clients to keep with the fashion house's original spirit. Dozens of candidates were being considered, but McCartney became the only choice when their scouts saw her first collection, with the vintage lace and tailoring and the celebrity fans like Kate Moss.

"I was actually beginning to gain recognition for designing a particular style of clothes in London. This is why the Chloé scouts came to see me. They liked my style. They liked my designs," she said, adding "Who on earth would buy clothes just because the designer was the daughter of a Beatle."

Before she signed the contract, she made it clear that her vegetarian principles, inherited from her mother, were non-negotiable, and that she would not work with fur or leather. Once this was agreed, she moved to Paris to establish herself at the headquarters on rue du Faubourg Saint-Honoré, and a year later she was joined by her close friend and assistant Phoebe Philo.

OPPOSITE Stella McCartney with models Kirsty Hume and Helena Christensen on the catwalk at the culmination of he[r] Autumn/Winter 1 collection.

As she planned out her debut show, knowing that the world's press would be watching keenly, Stella wondered whether she should take advantage of the marketing opportunity, and "do it outside at the Eiffel Tower with helicopters." It wasn't needed – she was on the front page of every London newspaper with her debut collection for Chloé.

Paul McCartney led the standing ovation at the end of the first show, with Gaby Aghion crying with emotion from the front row. Suzy Menkes said Stella, with her "girlish freshness" of design had "confounded the cynics who said that she had been hired only for her name" and that, following in Lagerfeld's giant footprints, she had "wisely sent out a simple, unpretentious show literally filled with little nothings: dresses as light as a scarf; wispy printed blouses with floaty flower-child sleeves; slithery negligee dresses, always with the dressmaking details." American buyers were similarly impressed, with the president of Bergdorf Goodman calling it "absolute perfection".

While she resisted trying to make her designs fit with the heritage of Chloé ("I never thought this dress needs another ruffle to make it more Chloé"), her sexy but structured tailoring proved that she was one of the hottest young designers in the world. Her second collection, Autumn/Winter 1998, featured skin-tight satin, zip details and floral embroidery, but it wasn't as warmly received, with *The New York Times* referring to it as "more London party girl than chic Parisian".

Her Spring/Summer 1999 collection took on board the criticism that some of her pieces were tacky, by introducing what would be a McCartney signature – using fun print motifs such as tropical beach prints and eagle heads, alongside her silk camisoles, petticoat dresses and good

OPPOSITE The hummingbird-print dress from Spring/Summer 1999 was the type of cheeky motif that became a hit item.

RIGHT A sexy but still retro design made from rhinestones from the Spring/Summer 2000 collection by Stella McCartney.

LEFT Modern glamour modelled by Tanga Moreau on the runway for the Autumn/Winter 1999 collection featuring a print of sea anemones and sequined cape. The ensemble was later worn by Madonna opposite.

OPPOSITE Madonna at the Chelsea Hotel, celebrating the opening of the new Chloé boutique in New York in September 1999.

tailoring. The show opened with a clip of Bill Clinton denying his affair with Monica Lewinsky. It was the topic on everyone's lips in 1998, and she considered it a perfect fit for her exploration of female sexuality.

Stella continued to push the boundaries of sexiness. For her Autumn/Winter 1999 collection, featuring figure-hugging denim, bustiers and sequins, she reportedly clashed with Chloé's president over how sheer and exposing her dresses would be. Spring/Summer 2000 was even more provocative, with supermodels including Gisele Bündchen revealing their oiled bodies in micro-minis, frayed white denim shorts and lurex bikinis. In the era of the recently launched *Sex and the City*, Stella's glamorous, liberated designs tapped into the zeitgeist.

"I like to explore the mechanics of the sexes through my work. I find the idea of a woman wearing a Savile Row tailored man's suit, with those secretive three-button cuffs and double vents, incredibly sexy," she said in an interview with the *Daily Telegraph* in 2000. "This is a very strange era for women. Women are powerful and this affects men and our relationships with men. We don't want to be pushed around, but at the same time we want to be powerful in our femininity."

She was also making an impact on Chloé's profitability. After six collections, sales had increased by 500 per cent and the fashion house was now as commercially successful as the big hitters like Gucci, Versace, Dior and Prada.

One of Stella's signatures was the horse motif, which was splashed across her must-have Spring/Summer 2001 collection, unveiled at the October 2000 Paris fashion Week. In mythology Chloé is an epithet for the fertility goddess Demeter, to whom horses were sacred, and Stella's

OPPOSITE Stella McCartney with Liv Tyler at the 2000 VH1/*Vogue* Fashion Awards, both wearing the horse motif from the Spring/Summ 2001 collection.

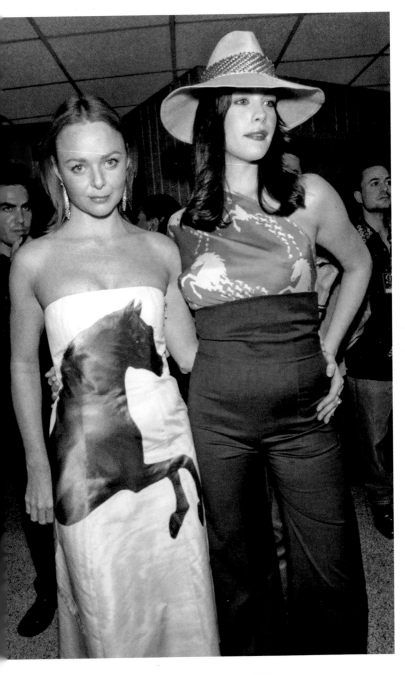

LEFT A fruit-inspired, saucy slogan for the Spring/Summer 2001 collection, which was the most celebrated of McCartney's tenure

OPPOSITE Raica Oliveira wearing the iconic horse-print dress by Stella McCartney for the Chloé Spring/Summer 2001 collection.

galloping horse represented the freedom of the Chloé girl. There were belted jackets with a horse on one shoulder, and an A-symmetrical slouchy dress with a huge horse's head printed on it. This same collection featured the cheeky fruit prints that would be much coveted – pineapples and strategically placed bananas on off-the-shoulder sweaters, and slashed swimsuits in acid yellow with pineapples on the front and back. Some of these sold-out pieces quickly became collector's items.

At the now iconic VH1/*Vogue* Fashion Awards on 20 October 2000, in New York, McCartney arrived with fellow rock star's daughter Liv Tyler, both brandishing the horse motif – Stella in a strapless white satin gown emblazoned with a huge image of a horse, and Liv in an aqua horse-print top and high-waisted trousers. Stella was named Designer of the Year, and was to be presented with the award by David Bowie, who pretended to have lost it – and Paul McCartney was there to hand it over instead. Rock royalty indeed.

Other cult items of her reign included hummingbird print baseball shirts from Spring/Summer 1999, the zodiac shirts from Autumn/Winter 2000, the sold-out diamond-encrusted heart sunglasses, and the Chloé varsity patches from Autumn/Winter 2001, which Bella Hadid was pictured wearing 20 years later.

In April 2001, after months of speculation, Stella McCartney announced that she was leaving Chloé so that she could set up her own label under the Gucci group. Her last collection for Chloé moved away from the kitsch, and while it was still nipple-baring, with well-cut hipsters and a bustier with a bat motif, it was dominated by a muted palette. It marked the end of a lucrative era under McCartney, which had completely switched around the maison's fortunes, but the next chapter would take it to an even starrier level.

OPPOSITE The pineapple swimsuit helped elevate the Spring/Summer 2001 collection to cult status, model here by Ana Claudia Michels.

The It
Focus

Becoming the must-have maison

When Stella McCartney announced her departure in 2000, the obvious choice as her successor was Phoebe Philo, who had been her confidante since they met at Central Saint Martins and her assistant at Chloé since 1998. She would be a young, culturally hip creative director for the new millennium.

There were hints that perhaps Stella and Phoebe had parted ways both as colleagues and friends, as Stella left to establish her own brand and Phoebe now slinked into the top job at Chloé.

"Stella changed a lot at Chloé and I totally respect her for that," said Phoebe in 2001. "I learnt a hell of a lot from her. You know, I'm quite spontaneous and she's into subtle detail and beautiful things and I'm sure that will come through in the way I design now."

Originally from Harrow on the Hill, a historic village on the outskirts of London, Phoebe rebelled against her middle-class upbringing as the daughter of an art dealer and chartered surveyor by skipping school, listening to ragga and decorating her fingers with sovereign rings. Phoebe met Stella while studying Womenswear at Central Saint Martins, with Phoebe in

OPPOSITE Phoebe Philo's Spring/Summer 2002 collection.

the year below, and the two would hang out at Portobello Road Market together, sourcing vintage fabrics and buttons. Phoebe helped her set up her own label, and when Stella landed the top job at Chloé, followed her to Paris a year later.

Phoebe was much more inspired by street style than Stella, and it's believed it was her influence that brought a youthful edge to the tailored suits and camisoles of Stella's collections. She was said to have been the one who put airbrushed tropical scenes, pineapples and slogans on T-shirts, and brought her cheeky style into the cultish sunglasses range.

For her first collection, Spring/Summer 2002, Phoebe aimed to prove she could take Chloé in a mature direction. "I'm not that ragga chick thing that everyone thinks I am," she said in June 2001, as she was forced to deny that she'd ever had dreadlocks. She planned out an "elegant but very sexy" collection which was inspired by Bianca Jagger, Talitha Getty and Brigitte Bardot in Saint-Tropez. It included delicious cream sweaters, scallop-edged jackets and tiny shorts (inspired by the scalloping in a 1960 collection), coral ruffled blouses, and fun touches such as a mesh top with monkeys climbing palm trees. It won universal praise, with predictions that some of its pieces, including her first It bag, the "Bracelet", inspired by a charm bracelet bought in Ibiza, would become cult items.

"Philo has kept Chloé's soft and womanly side, while making dresses slightly more grown up and elegant than the former raunchy rock chick image," wrote Suzy Menkes.

As with Stella, Phoebe's own personal style was praised – and this effortless chic was translated into Chloé's floaty blouses and dresses. For Spring/Summer 2003 she continued the feminine sophistication of her debut, with black draped minidresses which Suzy Menkes compared to Karl Lagerfeld in the early 1970s, broderie anglaise dresses and blouses, jackets studded with pearl

OPPOSITE The Bracelet, from Spring/Summer 2002, was the first Chloé "It" bag, inspired by a charm bracelet that Phoebe Philo sourced in Ibiza.

or with fringing, and elaborate necklaces like breastplates. Philo told reporters: "It's Chloé sexy, which is not vulgar, not cheap, but refined, and hot and raunchy. This collection is all about finding great things to wear."

In 2002 Chloé posted consolidated sales of $162 million, proving that profits were soaring under Phoebe, as she introduced a number of cult favourites and courted the new breed of It girls and paparazzi targets, whose images were disseminated widely in gossip magazines and the new online platforms.

Phoebe's most influential collection at Chloé was the Spring/Summer 2004 collection, and saw *The New York Times* referring to her as "the Chanel of her generation". A floaty green chiffon dress cinched with a brown belt encapsulated the free-spirited nature of this collection, which moved away from the tomboy, streetwear influence of previous shows to a summery 1970s feel. It was a dress that spoke for the feverish adoption of boho style, as worn by Sienna Miller, a devoted fan of the maison. Blue Farrier, a member of the Chloé team, spoke to *Vogue* in 2005: "Instead of trying to do a look with jeans, a boot, and a jacket, there was a sense of loving a very beautiful dress. But something easy. How Phoebe would like to wear a dress."

Bananas were the major theme of the collection, after Phoebe was inspired by a photo of Kate Moss in a vintage banana print top and asked stylist Bay Garnett if she could borrow it. The prints appeared on long-sleeve tops (which Lily Allen revived in an Instagram selfie), on swimsuits with cut-out panels and on chain-mail leather shoulder bags. As Phoebe told *Vogue*: "During the late seventies, cotton T-shirts with bright stripes or fun characters on them were a part of every girl's wardrobe! We selected bright colors, especially green and yellow, so the banana print became obvious."

OPPOSITE Chloé's Autumn/Winter 2003 collection on model Natalia Vodianova. The boho style perfectly encapsulated the Noughties generation.

OPPOSITE The
ana print, here
delled by Michelle
es, was the cult
ign from Phoebe
o's Spring/
mmer 2004 show.
as inspired by a
oto of Kate Moss
vintage top.

HT With its
ty green chiffon
ched with a
t, Phoebe Philo
ght to elevate
simplicity of a
utiful dress for
Spring/Summer
4 collection,
n here by Dewi
egen.

LEFT Cameron
Russell walking
in Phoebe Philo's
Spring/Summer
2005 collection fo
Chloé.

OPPOSITE Daria
Werbowy in a gree
satin and rhinesto
dress for the Sprir
Summer 2005
collection.

Because of McCartney's resistance to using leather, bags hadn't been much of a feature of her collections. However, in tune with this celebrity-obsessed era, Phoebe tapped into a consumer desire to own the latest "hot" item. In late 2004 she launched the Paddington bag, which was an instant smash. The slouchy leather bag featured an oversized padlock, inspired by a beautiful one she had, asserting the codes of luxury in an exaggerated way, and became a must-have among fashionistas, including Nicole Richie, Kate Bosworth and Halle Berry. The Chloé Silverado, with a hippie-chic flavour, was in the spirit of vintage bags, with antique golden rivets, whipstitched top handles, and side flap pockets. There were lengthy waits to try to get hold of these bags, and stories of bringing in extra security at London's Chloé stores to prepare for the frenzy. In 2005, British *Vogue* described the bag, with its vintage scruffiness, as "ideal for the not-so-precious. It's well-suited to take a battering and destined to improve with age."

With her slouchy "boyfriend" trousers, striped ponchos and delicate lace blouses, Phoebe's Autumn/Winter 2004 show was described by André Leon Talley as her best yet. He praised her for being master of the modern vintage: "She has made Chloé soar in a way it has not soared since the seventies, when Karl Lagerfeld first made the house one of fashion's most wanted labels."

WWD agreed about the power she was wielding, not just for Chloé but for fashion. In a 10 October 2005 article, they called her "one of the hottest, most-copied designers in fashion, having infused girlish dressing with a whole new savvy." That same year she was named British Designer of the Year at the British Fashion Awards. The Autumn/Winter 2005 collection was completed by her team while she was on maternity leave, but despite her absence it featured some of her signatures – the lace blouses and loose tailored trousers, and a nod to Lagerfeld with a triangle-print white dress similar to one from his Spring/Summer 1993 collection.

OPPOSITE Kate Bosworth with one arm on Orlando Bloom, the other on her Paddington bag in 2005 in Sydney, Australia.

In January 2006 Phoebe announced that she was leaving Chloé to spend more time with her family. The news caused shockwaves throughout the fashion world, with fears that this change would impact on the winning streak of the maison, which had been so successful over the past few years. Her final collection, Spring/Summer 2006, was a breezy swansong, with clean lines, white gowns, and satin skirt and shirt combinations.

With Phoebe's absence, the in-house design team at Chloé, which included Yvan Mispelaere, Blue Farrier and Adrian Appiolaza, completed the Autumn/Winter 2006 collection. The Australian model Gemma Ward opened the show, wearing a voluminous brown wool coat with large buttons, followed by prim tunics and khaki and oatmeal pinafore dresses, reminiscent of schoolgirl uniforms, and a delicate white laser-cut leather Empire-line dress.

Front-row guest Nathalie Rykiel, who designed Sonia Rykiel with her mother, said: "I think the team did an amazing job because they managed to continue something that is totally coherent with the identity of the brand. There was a lightness, a freshness, the shoes were amazing and there were very, very charming dresses which one wants to wear."

Following Philo's departure, avant-garde Swedish designer Paulo Melim Andersson, coming from Marni, stepped into her shoes, choosing modern over vintage, "clean but not minimal", and describing his Chloé girl as "funny, but angry-funny". Phoebe Philo was a hard act to follow, as her incredible popularity had elevated Chloé to the must-have fashion house of celebrities and hip urbanites. His debut collection, for Autumn/Winter 2007, was predominantly black and orange, with a monochrome graphic print dress and low-waisted translucent dresses, but it was considered more aggressive rather than girlish. As *Vogue* wrote: "Andersson's challenge is to maintain Chloé's

OPPOSITE Phoebe Philo's final collection for Chloé, Spring/Summer 2006, with its shirt and skirt combinations.

LEFT The crisp white dresses with frills and cutwork details, from Spring Summer 2006.

OPPOSITE Models backstage at the Spring/Summer 2007 show, which was curated by the studio team following Phoebe Philo's departure.

minance of the dirty-pretty-thing market." Alongside
any other fashion journalists, *The New York Times*' Cintra
Wilson was not convinced. When reviewing his collection in
September 2007, she said: "His boxy, conservative lines don't
embrace free, youthful rebellion so much as they suggest that
Chloé, in a rut of depression and weight gain, is becoming a
square…"

The *International Herald Tribune* described Andersson's
Autumn/Winter 2008 as "awkward", despite the return to
the 1970s with floral print chiffon tea dresses and translucent
beaded gowns. After only three collections, Andersson's tenure
came to an end when he was asked to step down. As Hadley
Freeman wrote in the *Guardian*: "The end, when it finally
came, was not surprising but a shame."

Andersson had failed to capture the essence of the Chloé girl, but hopes were high when British designer Hannah MacGibbon stepped in as creative director in March 2008. Graduating from Central Saint Martins in 1996, she was hired five years later as assistant to Phoebe Philo, and with her understanding of what had made the fashion house so popular she was the obvious choice. Soon after her appointment, she helped to launch Chloé Parfum in spring 2008, and showed her debut collection for Spring/Summer 2009. It was muted but breezy – with neutral white, cream, camel, olive and splashes of lemon for her jumpsuits, scallop-edged coats and one-shoulder dresses. The standout item was a pair of copper balloon pants. Working under the pressure of a global recession, she created designs that were edgy-romantic, luxury bohemian, with innovations including blanket coats and thigh-high suede boots. "I think everyone's got a bit of Chloé inside her," she told Suzy Menkes. "That's what I love: realness. And I think I am quite real."

Her following collections were said to have toughened up the look of Chloé, moving away from the sugary to the hard edge of the 1970s, and inspired by icons like Lauren Hutton, with her desert-toned trousers and shirts, relaxed jumpsuits and caramel satin blouses. Spring/Summer 2011 was a welcome return to lightness, with minimalist silhouettes including draped Grecian dresses, clean white blouses and ballet-style tulle skirts.

Her final collection for Chloé, for Autumn/Winter 2011, led with python prints. There were snakeskin blouses and dresses, on shoes and accessories, alongside denim skirts and patchwork ponchos. With Hannah MacGibbon's contract ending, and with an awareness that the reception to her collections was muted, no one was surprised that in 2011 she was replaced by a new visionary.

OPPOSITE Hannah MacGibbon's Spring/Summer 2009 collection, showcased in Miami Beach.

PPOSITE The
ring/Summer 2011
ection was all
out lightness and
mmering fabrics.

GHT A snakeskin-
nt high-necked
ss at the
tumn/Winter
2 presentation
aris.

Bringing Past
Into Future

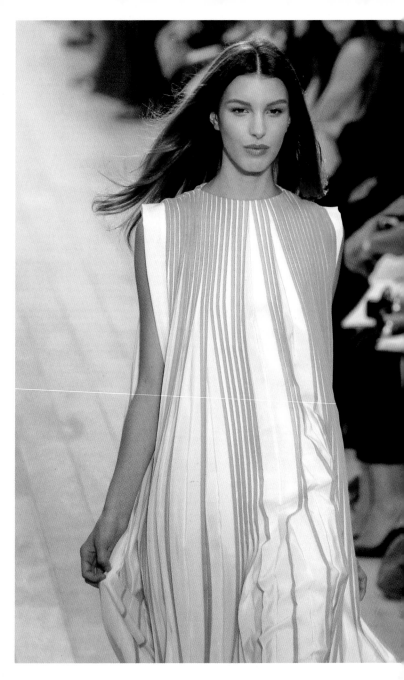

Finding power in femininity

A new era at Chloé was revealed when Clare Waight Keller took over as creative director in 2011. The Birmingham-born designer fell in love with fashion through witnessing subcultures like punks and goths as she was growing up, and with a love for flicking through the pages of *Vogue* to take her to new realms.

She honed her sense of minimalism working for Calvin Klein in New York in the 1990s, and from there she went to Gucci, where she worked under Tom Ford. After five years, she returned to Britain to work as creative director for Pringle of Scotland.

Now that she was at Chloé, she chose to balance the "girly" and "flirty" with something cooler and more modern. "The Chloé woman is someone empowered by being feminine," she said, and so she brought a new attitude to the fashion house. Her first collection, for Spring/Summer 2012, was a perfect blend of the light ice-cream palette that had come to define Chloé, along with floral embroideries, colourful pleating and tailoring.

OPPOSITE The Spring/Summer 2012 collection included the light ice-cream palette now forever associated with Chloé, and colourful pleating.

Clare Waight Keller was, like Stella McCartney and Phoebe Philo before her, a British woman living and working in Paris, and her aim for her second collection, Autumn/Winter 2012, was to mix English sportswear with Parisian chic. Her slouchy trousers, casual jumpsuits and jackets were embraced by Hollywood A-listers like Gwyneth Paltrow, Cate Blanchett and Victoria Beckham, who admired the off-duty look of her clothes – the light fabrics, the soft layering, the contrast with the sturdy boots. "By adding boyish elements, it stops you tripping into that overly girlie territory. It's bringing that mix together that creates tension and makes it more modern and easier," she said.

To mark 60 years of Chloé, a celebratory show was held at the end of September 2012, with a Spring/Summer 2013 collection that looked to the future and which featured intricate layers of pleats, and short boxy tops over longer layers. "I played a lot with proportions and layers – the idea of a T-shirt broken up with different proposals," Clare said backstage, referring to what she described as "soft volumes". She also used silver arrows, from the Karl era, to add a metallic line on white, the dominant colour in the collection.

Her Spring/Summer 2014 collection of cool designs were considered her best yet, with the wow factor being the light-as-air micro-pleats in white silk dresses and khaki silk pants with loose ankle ties. The micro-pleating took two months of planning to work out the dimensions and structure so that they looked fresh and had bounce. This collection was also praised for the burnished khaki leather pants and blue crochet lace dresses, and the earthy palette inspired by the arid climates of California and the Mediterranean. "That's where the desert-like colour palette came in and the dry fabrics, the sense of having something very light on the skin without being transparent," she said. Phoebe Philo may have created the Paddington Bag, but in

OPPOSITE The flor embroidery was a standout at Clare Waight Keller's det collection for Sprir Summer 2012.

2014 Waight Keller introduced the Drew shoulder bag – which quickly became the latest must-have, featuring a curved saddle shape, a rectangular flap and a gold clasp.

In 2013 92-year-old Gaby Aghion was honoured with the Chevalier of the order of the Legion of Honour, the highest civilian award given in France, acknowledging those who have made an outstanding contribution. She was presented with the medal by French culture and communications minister Aurélie Filippetti, who praised her for making fashion accessible, and shifting away from elite couture to more egalitarian ready-to-wear. Gaby still possessed the twinkling eyes, enthusiasm and passion from when she first conceived the idea of Chloé in her apartment in Paris. A year later, on 27 September 2014, she passed away at the age of 93.

ABOVE The Chloé
Drew bag in jade
green leather.
This design was
introduced by Clare
Waight Keller in
2014.

OPPOSITE Model
Mily Reuter carried
the mini cross-body
Faye bag, during
Waight Keller's
Spring/Summer 2015
show.

It was a heavy burden for Clare to hold her Spring/Summer 2015 show the day after the news of Gaby's death broke. She dedicated the show to her memory: the lacy baby-doll dresses, flowing crepes that represented the "flou", or fluid clothes, favoured by Gaby, and neat tailored shorts with blouses and jackets, which summed up the bohemian ethos of the maison. She moved towards technicolour for her Spring/Summer 2016 show, with flowing rainbow dresses and sporty tracksuit pants, and for Autumn/Winter 2017 she was inspired by 1970s motorcyclist adventurer Anne-France Dautheville for her trippy hippie dresses, huge and enveloping desert capes, sheepskin jackets and leather trousers.

Clare Waight Keller's final collection was held in March 2017. Marianne Faithfull and, in a sheer white diaphanous gown, Solange Knowles were in the front row to witness her psychedelic designs which played with a mix of eras from Chloé. They combined the spirit of Gaby Aghion and her love of "le flou" with Viennese Secession-inspired prints that Lagerfeld

created in the 1970s. There were leather pinafores over paisley-pattern pussy-bow blouses, Peter Pan dresses, and a black and white art nouveau print dress.

Waight Keller had successfully boosted sales with her wearable pieces and hit accessories. She introduced countless It bags, including the Drew, Nile, Faye and the Pixie. Now that she was moving to Givenchy, where she would be creative director between 2017 and 2020, a replacement was sought.

Parisian-born Natacha Ramsay-Levi was named as the new creative director in March 2017 – the first Frenchwoman to be in creative control of Chloé since Martine Sitbon in 1987. Edgy and avant-garde, she was inspired by the street style she grew up with on the Left Bank. Her parents worked in the literary world, and after studying history she went to the fashion school Studio Berçot in 2000. She began her career in fashion because she "really wanted to be a Balenciaga girl: young, cool, androgynous".

Natacha gained her entrance into the business as an intern for Nicolas Ghesquière in 2002, and worked under him, as artistic director of Balenciaga and Louis Vuitton, for 15 years. She said: "He helped me understand that being a fashion designer is not only to design clothes, it is to develop a 360-degree vision of everything." He taught her to create with a democratic touch, and she was struck by his equal love for classical paintings and the music of Mariah Carey. She was trained in modernism and futuristic cool, almost the opposite of what has been described as Chloé's aura of "the boho-girl-running-through-Provence".

As an historian, Natacha pored over the Chloé archives to copy prints from Lagerfeld's collections, and to bring back the horse motifs from Stella McCartney. While playing with the past, she also looked to the future, as she aimed, she said, "to give women the possibility of showing their strength, not

OPPOSITE A long dress in sunray-pleated knit, alternating white and navy stripes at the Spring/Summer 2017 show.

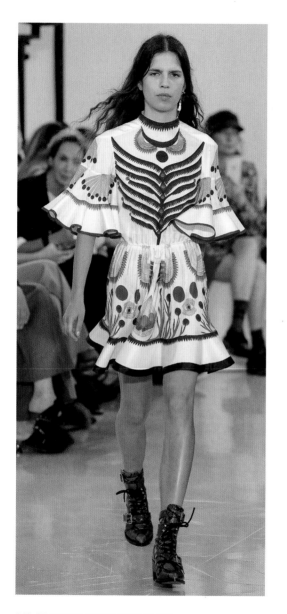

their power." For her debut Spring/Summer 2018 collection she followed Lagerfeld's lead with printed silk dresses, featuring auspicious hands and eyes created by Indian artist Rithika Merchant.

Bohemian festival chic was the theme of the Spring/Summer 2019 collection, which Natacha referred to as "hippie modernism", with eclectic prints, loose dresses and an ombré T-shirt with raised hands that would be perfect for holidays in Ibiza or Goa. The following year she shifted in her style to the other side of the Chloé coin, with an urban minimalism, featuring pinstripe trousers, loose dresses with gentle pleated skirts and clean white blouses. It was the balance that Chloé traditionally sought – that of "le flou" and of the tailoring and soft blouses.

Having worked to the constraints of the global Covid-19 pandemic, Natacha decided to leave Chloé and the announcement was made in December 2020. Gabriela Hearst's appointment as creative director would mark a further shift for Chloé, this time by following a more sustainable model.

Gabriela Hearst grew up riding horses and surrounded by livestock on her family's cattle ranch in Uruguay. Raised with a conscientiousness around clothing being made to last, she was committed to sustainability and transparency in the luxury supply chain.

She chose to use recycled cashmere and upcycled "deadstock" – the fabric leftovers from previous collections that would normally be discarded – and other sustainable materials to ensure her collections were as green as possible.

Her first collection, for Autumn/Winter 2021, was presented digitally in March 2021, due to the ongoing pandemic, and the date coincided with the 100th birthday of Gaby Aghion. Gabriela was conscious of the heritage she was taking on and she considered it essential to her debut that she pay tribute

OPPOSITE Boho teamed with tough boots for Spring/Summer 2018 in Paris. This print was created with the artist Rithika Merchant.

OPPOSITE Geometric patterns contrast with lace and metallic touches for Autumn/Winter 2018 in Paris.

LEFT Gwyneth Paltrow wearing a *Valley of the Dolls* inspired Chloé maxi-dress for the 2019 Met Gala

Chloé's founder. Guests were taken on a journey through fashion and Lagerfeld's old Left Bank haunts, travelling from Brasserie Lipp and along the cobbled streets to the Café de Flore, where the first Chloé shows took place.

Gabriela mixed flowing dresses and upcycled second hand with bags with her own South American heritage of striped ponchos, and, as a finale, the "puffcho" – a Bordeaux-striped blanket poncho with a high puffer collar. There were flowing Edwardian-style white dresses, patchwork leather coats, moonbooties with linings made from recycled cashmere, and an inside-out version of a Sheltersuit made from upcycled silks, which could be turned into a sleeping bag for the homeless. She worked with the non-profit foundation to make 1,000 traditional backpacks from deadstock. In 2021, Chloé became the first luxury brand to be a Certified B Corporation.

In a *New York Times* feature in March 2021, entitled, "The Chloé girl has grown up and grown a social conscience", Vanessa Friedman described the new "circular economy" look of Chloé under Gabriela Hearst.

"A figure emerges from the Brasserie Lipp, the famous old Parisian restaurant where Apollinaire and Cocteau once dined, striding onto the cobblestones of a dimly lit, deserted street in the protective embrace of a striped knit. It is half poncho, half puffer, with the sweep of a Musketeers cape. Caught on film, she is serving not croque-madame, but rather notice to the world: There's a new Chloé girl in town."

Gabriela's Spring/Summer 2022 collection further pushed the green credentials. For Autumn/Winter 2022, she focused on hope and rewilding. Her collection revealed the positives in combating climate change, such as bags and wraps portraying forest fires, with the reverse featuring climate successes, such as polar bears against ice caps. As Chloé has gone through extraordinary change across more than 70 years of history, the maison entered a new era of climate consciousness under Gabriela Hearst.

In October 2023, Chemena Kamali was appointed as the new creative director, opening an exciting new chapter for the Maison, given her passion for the brand's heritage and her strong connection to Chloé. Having started her collaboration with the Maison with an internship during Phoebe's era, she declared, "my heart has always been Chloé's. It has been since I stepped through its doors more than 20 years ago." Kamali's first collection was highly acclaimed during Paris Fashion Week

OPPOSITE Olivia Wilde at the 2023 Met Gala, wearing a tribute to Karl Lagerfeld: a reinterpretation of the iconic Angkor dress (commonly called the violin dress) in a longer version than the original.

RIGHT Long dresses constructed from multi-coloured patchwork of nappa leather, Spring/Summer 2022.

OPPOSITE Amber Valletta in a multi-coloured quilted silk crepe vest sewn by the Gee's Bend Quilters for Autumn/Winter 2022.

in March 2024, and ranked as the top collection of Fall 2024 shown during the fashion weeks by *WWD*, with the journalist Miles Socha writing "Chemena Kamali did a bang-up job with her runway debut for Chloé, capturing the brand's sunny nonchalance, natural femininity and youthful elan, while also injecting some of the playfulness Karl Lagerfeld plied during two brand-defining tenures."

Since its very foundation, the ethos of Chloé was to look to the future, with Gaby Aghion designing dresses to suit the fashion-conscious but busy modern woman. As well as being a female-led fashion house, it shared a similar ethos to Coco Chanel in creating clothing to help women navigate their lives. The brand became a place for young creatives to thrive and explore their visions: from the team of designers in the 1960s to the star designers who helped make Chloé a favourite among bright young things with their It items – the Paddington bag, as well as the Drew and Marcie, the Susanna boots, the horse motifs, and the banana print tops. Alongside Karl Lagerfeld's cult designs and bohemian whimsy, they all helped shape the Chloé woman into a cool, edgy free spirit.

Index

Credits

The publishers would like to thank the following sources for their kind permission to reproduce the pictures in this book.

© APF Lewandowski-Beylard: 8 (top left)

Bridgeman Images: 22; /AGIP 35, 36; /SZ Photo/Max Scheler 34

Getty Images: Bassignac/BUU/Gamma-Rapho via Getty Images 118, 119; /Gustavo Caballero 129; /Stephane Cardinale/Sygma via Getty Images 90, 106, 115; /Dominique Charriau/WireImage 147; /Mike Coppola 153; /Robert Doisneau/Gamma-Rapho/ Getty Images 26; /Steve Eichner/WWD/ Penske Media via Getty Images 103; /Estrop 145, 148; /Fairchild Archive/WWD/Penske Media via Getty Images 16, 60, 94-95, 121, 139; /Giovanni Giannoni/Penske Media via Getty Images 87, 97, 116; /Reginald Gray/ WWD/Penske Media via Getty Images 39, 42, 45, 50; /Pierre Guillaud/AFP 74; / Francois Guillot/AFP via Getty Images 125, 126, 137; /Keystone-France/Gamma-Rapho via Getty Images 12, 25, 29; /KMazur/ WireImage 105; /Thierry Orban/Sygma 100-101, 102; /Dominique Maître/WWD/ Penske Media via Getty Images 120; / Michel Maurou/WWD/Penske Media 61, 62, 63, 75, 76; /Guy Marineau/WWD/

Penske Media via Getty Images 53, 57, 58, 64, 65, 67;/Michel Maurou/WWD/Penske Media via Getty Images 47; /Antonio de Moraes Barros Filho/WireImage 131, 134, 140, 141;/Pat/Arnal/Gamma-Rapho via Getty Images 93; /Jean-Claude Sauer/Paris Match via Getty Images 32; /Pascal Le Segretain 130, 154; /Daniel Simon/Gamma Rapho via Getty Images 68, 69, 72, 81, 85, 98; /Antonello Trio 144; /Underwood Archives 55; /Pierre Verdy/AFP via Getty Images 107, 112; /Christian Vierig 142; / Victor Virgile/Gamma-Rapho via Getty Images 78, 79, 82, 84, 109, 138, 143, 150, 155; /Angela Weiss/AFP 151; /WWD/ Penske Media via Getty Images 40-41, 54; /David Yoder/WWD/Penske Media via Getty Images 127

Imaged by Heritage Auctions, HA.com: 8 (top left)

Jean-Luce Huré: 46, 48, 51, 66

Nicolas Norblin: 8 (top right)

Scala Archives: RMN-Grand Palais /Dist. Photo SCALA, Florence 37

Shutterstock: 8 (top right); /FashionStock. com 6; /Ross Hodgson 123